Dinosaurs

Mosasaurus

by Julie Murray

1

Dash!
LEVELED READERS
An Imprint of Abdo Zoom • abdobooks.com

Dash!
LEVELED READERS

Level 1 – Beginning
Short and simple sentences with familiar words or patterns for children who are beginning to understand how letters and sounds go together.

Level 2 – Emerging
Longer words and sentences with more complex language patterns for readers who are practicing common words and letter sounds.

Level 3 – Transitional
More developed language and vocabulary for readers who are becoming more independent.

THIS BOOK CONTAINS RECYCLED MATERIALS

abdobooks.com

Published by Abdo Zoom, a division of ABDO, PO Box 398166, Minneapolis, Minnesota 55439.

Printed in the United States of America, North Mankato, Minnesota.
052024
092024

Photo Credits: Alamy, Getty Images, Shutterstock
Production Contributors: Kenny Abdo, Jennie Forsberg, Grace Hansen, John Hansen
Design Contributors: Neil Klinepier

Library of Congress Control Number: 2023948544

Publisher's Cataloging in Publication Data

Names: Murray, Julie, author.
Title: Mosasaurus / by Julie Murray
Description: Minneapolis, Minnesota : Abdo Zoom, 2025 | Series: Dinosaurs | Includes online resources and index.
Identifiers: ISBN 9781098285456 (lib. bdg.) | ISBN 9781098286156 (ebook) | ISBN 9781098286507 (Read-to-me eBook)
Subjects: LCSH: Dinosaurs--Juvenile literature. | Mosasaurus--Juvenile literature. | Prehistoric animals--Juvenile literature. | Paleontology--Juvenile literature. | Extinct animals--Juvenile literature.
Classification: DDC 567.9--dc23

Table of Contents

Mosasaurus

Mosasaurus was not a dinosaur. It was a **marine** reptile.

It lived 70 million years ago.
It ruled **prehistoric** seas.

It swam near the water's surface. It came up to breathe.

Mosasaurus was huge! It could grow up to 60 feet (18.3 m) long.

It had two sets of fins. Its tail was long and powerful.

It had a big head. The head was four feet (1.2 m) long!

Mosasaurus had many sharp teeth. It could open its mouth wide to catch its **prey**.

It ate fish, birds, and turtles.
It also ate sharks!

The first Mosasaurus **fossil** was found in 1764 in the Netherlands.

More Facts

- *Mosasaurus* means "lizard of the Meuse River." The first **fossil** was found near the Meuse River.
- Mosasaurus could swim up to 30 miles per hour (48 kph).
- Some scientists believe that Mosasaurus is a relative of snakes and monitor lizards.

Glossary

fossil – the remains or trace of a living animal or plant from a long time ago. Fossils are found embedded in earth or rock.

marine – living in the sea.

prehistoric – belonging to a period of time before written history.

prey – an animal hunted by another animal for food.

Index

Online Resources

Booklinks
NONFICTION NETWORK
FREE! ONLINE NONFICTION RESOURCES

To learn more about Mosasaurus, please visit **abdobooklinks.com** or scan this QR code. These links are routinely monitored and updated to provide the most current information available.